For my nephew Scott

電視是我的！

THE TV IS MINE!

文 Jill McDougall

圖 余麗婷

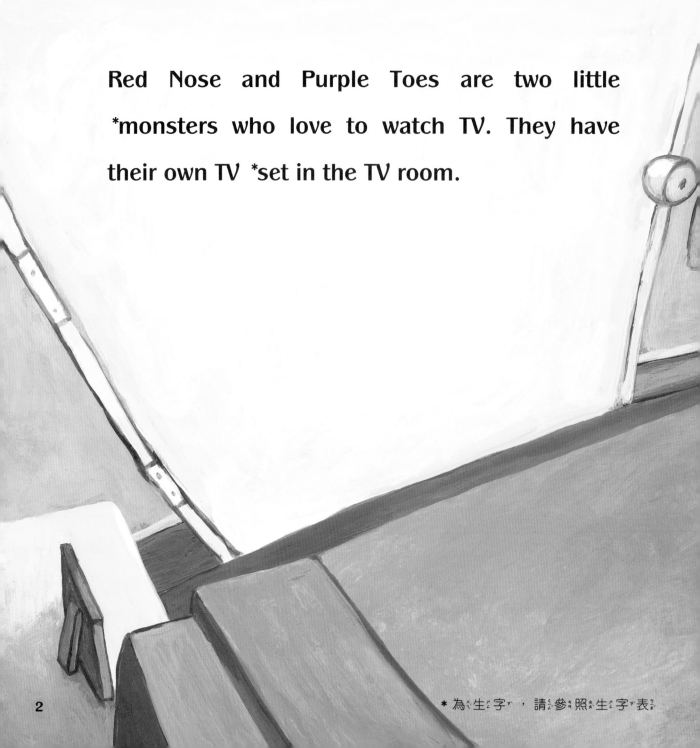

Red Nose and Purple Toes are two little
*monsters who love to watch TV. They have
their own TV *set in the TV room.

*為生字，請參照生字表

Red Nose likes to watch cartoons. Purple Toes likes

to watch soccer.

"I want to watch Mighty Mouse," says Red Nose.

Click! She *puts the TV on *Channel 9.

"I want to watch the World Cup," says Purple Toes.

Click! He puts the TV on Channel 10.

"Mighty Mouse!" says Red Nose.

Click! She puts the TV back on Channel 9.

"World Cup!" says Purple Toes.

Click! He puts the TV back on Channel 10.

"MIGHTY MOUSE!"

Click!

"WORLD CUP!"

Click!

When Purple Toes goes to get a *drink, Red Nose changes the TV back to "Mighty Mouse." Then she *locks the door.

"Let me in," *yells Purple Toes.

"Go away," yells Red Nose.

Purple Toes climbs in the window.

Click! He changes the TV to Channel 10.

Red Nose is *grumpy. She goes to watch TV in the *family room. But Ma Monster is watching a garden show.

Red Nose goes to watch TV in the kitchen. But Pa Monster is watching a show about cars.

Red Nose goes to bed feeling very grumpy.

In the middle of the night, Red Nose has an idea.

She *creeps into the TV room. She *presses lots of

buttons on the TV. Now it doesn't *work at all.

Then Red Nose creeps into the family room. She presses lots of buttons on the TV. Now *that* TV doesn't work at all.

Red Nose creeps into the kitchen. She presses lots of buttons on the TV. Now *that* TV doesn't work. "There," says Red Nose. "Now no one can watch TV."

The next day, Purple Toes goes to the TV room to watch soccer. "The TV isn't working," he says.

So Purple Toes goes outside with his soccer ball.

Ma Monster goes to the family room to watch her garden show. "The TV isn't working," she says.

So Ma Monster goes outside and works in her garden.

22

Pa Monster goes to the kitchen to watch his car show. "The TV isn't working," he says. So Pa Monster goes outside and *works on his car.

Purple Toes has fun playing soccer.

Ma Monster has fun working in her garden.

Pa Monster has fun working on his car.

But Red Nose has no fun at all. She goes to school feeling grumpy.

And she comes home feeling grumpy.

Red Nose goes to the TV room. Maybe she can fix the TV?

But the TV is not there.

She goes to the family room.

No TV.

She goes to the kitchen.

No TV.

"We don't need TV any more," says Ma Monster. "We can have fun without it."

That night the monster family has dinner in the garden. It is fun.

Then they play a *chasing game. That is fun too!

31

生字表

family room　　家庭娛樂室（家人聚在一起並且放鬆的地方，在這裡可以玩遊戲、看電視等）

p. 16 creep [krip] *v.* 躡手躡腳的走

press [prɛs] *v.* 按、壓

work [wɝk] *v.* 運轉、運作

p. 25 work on　　保養、修理

p. 30 chase [tʃes] *v.* 追逐

（詞性以縮寫表示：*n.*名詞，*v.*動詞，*adj.*形容詞）

電視是我的！

紅鼻子和紫腳趾是兩隻愛看電視的小怪獸。他們在電視間裡有屬於他們兩個的電視機。

紅鼻子喜歡看卡通。紫腳趾喜歡看足球。

紅鼻子說：「我要看太空飛鼠。」

喀嚓！她把電視轉到第九台。

紫腳趾說：「我要看世界盃足球賽。」

喀嚓！他把電視轉到第十台。

紅鼻子說：「看太空飛鼠！」

喀嚓！她把電視轉回第九台。

紫腳趾說：「看世界盃足球賽！」

喀嚓！他把電視轉回第十台。

「太空飛鼠！」

喀嚓！

「世界盃足球賽！」

喀嚓！

當紫腳趾去拿飲料的時候，紅鼻子把電視轉回「太空飛鼠」，然後把門鎖了起來。

紫腳趾大叫：「讓我進去！」

紅鼻子大喊：「走開啦！」

紫腳趾從窗戶爬了進來。

喀嚓！他把電視轉到第十台。

紅鼻子很生氣！她到娛樂室去看電視，但是怪獸媽媽在看園藝節目。

紅鼻子到廚房去看電視，但是怪獸爸爸在看汽車節目。

紅鼻子只好很不高興的上床睡覺。

半夜的時候，

紅鼻子想到一個點子。

她偷偷溜進電視間裡，按了一大堆電視上的按鈕，結果電視壞掉了。

然後紅鼻子溜進娛樂室裡，按了一大堆電

視上的按鈕，結果這台電視也壞掉了。

最後紅鼻子溜進廚房裡，按了一大堆電視上的按鈕，結果這台電視也壞掉了。

紅鼻子說：「好了，現在沒有人可以看電視了。」

第二天，紫腳趾到電視間看足球。

他說：「電視壞掉了。」

所以紫腳趾就到外面去踢足球。

怪獸媽媽到娛樂室看園藝節目。

她說：「電視壞掉了。」

所以怪獸媽媽就到外面花園裡整理花草。

怪獸爸爸到廚房看汽車節目。

他說：「電視壞掉了。」

所以怪獸爸爸就去外面保養他的車子。

紫腳趾踢足球玩得很開心。

怪獸媽媽在花園整理花草很開心。

怪獸爸爸保養他的車子也很開心。

但是紅鼻子卻一點也不開心。她很不高興的去上學，又很不高興的回家。

紅鼻子走到電視間裡，說不定她可以把電視修好？

但是電視不在那裡。

她到娛樂室去。

電視不在那裡。

她到廚房去。

電視也不在那裡。

怪獸媽媽說：「我們再也不需要電視囉。沒有電視，我們也可以過得很開心。」

那天晚上，怪獸一家人在花園裡吃晚餐。

他們覺得很有趣。

然後，他們一起玩追逐遊戲。他們覺得這也很有趣。

故事中的怪獸家庭不看電視了，他們找到了其他的樂趣喔！

現在他們要在以下五個房間玩捉迷藏：

TV room, family room, kitchen, Pa and Ma Monster's room, Red Nose and Purple Toes' room。你能不能依照右頁的敘述，找出他們各自躲在哪個房間呢？

（提示：有電視的房間有 TV room, family room, kitchen）

① All of the monsters are in different rooms.

② Red Nose is not in her room. She is in a room with no TV.

③ Pa Monster is not in the family room and kitchen. He is in a room with a TV.

④ Ma Monster is not in the kitchen. She is in a room with a TV.

⑤ Purple Toes is in a room with a TV.

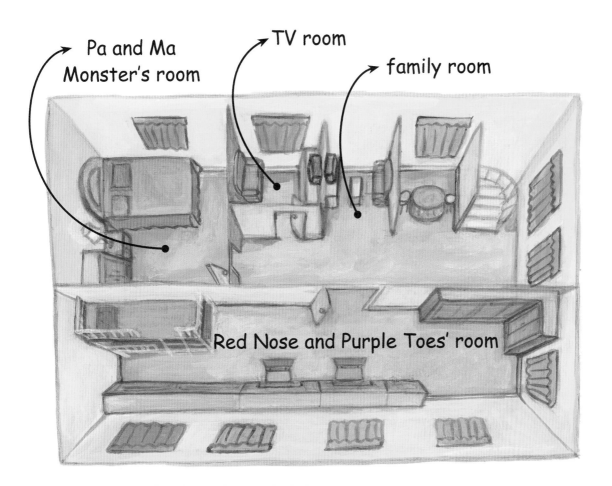

Pa and Ma Monster's room

TV room

family room

Red Nose and Purple Toes' room

看完了小怪獸的故事，是不是覺得很有趣呢？請看下面的圖片，聽 CD 的第四首，跟著一起唸，試著在空格填入適當的文字，多唸幾次，你就可以把這個故事說給別人聽囉！

1

Red Nose wants to watch Mighty Mouse.

She puts the TV on Channel 9.

Purple Toes _____ to _____ World Cup.

He _____ the TV _____ Channel 10.

2

3

4

Red Nose goes to other rooms to watch TV, but Ma Monster is watching a garden show in the family room.

Pa Monster is _____ a car show in the _____.

Red Nose has no TV to watch.

5

6

Red Nose creeps into the family room.

She presses lots of buttons on the TV.

Red Nose _____ into the kitchen.

She _____ lots of _____ on the TV.

Now the TVs don't work at all.

7

8

Ma Monster has fun working in the garden.

Pa Monster has fun _____ on his car.

Purple Toes _____ _____ playing soccer.

And they have fun playing a chasing game.

Now they all have fun without the TVs.

p. 45　working, has fun
p. 44　creeps, presses, buttons
p. 43　watching, kitchen
p. 42　wants, watch, puts, on

2. 怪獸家族又做了哪些事？

Purple Toes is in the kitchen.
Ma Monster is in the family room.
Pa Monster is in the TV room.
Red Nose is in Pa and Ma Monster's room.

1. 怪獸家族各在哪一個房間？

提示答案：

作者簡介

JILL MCDOUGALL lives in a cottage by the sea in South Australia. She has been a writer ever since she could hold a pencil and has written over ninety books for children. Her stories and poems are published in countries all around the world from the USA to Sweden to South Africa. Jill is also a teacher, an animal lover and a keen organic gardener.

Jill 目前住在澳洲南部海邊的一棟小屋裡。從她學會握筆的時候，她就是一位作家了，而她寫給兒童的作品已經超過九十本。從美國到瑞典，甚至南非，都能看到她出版的詩作及故事。Jill 同時也是一位老師、動物愛好者和愛好有機作物的園藝家。

繪者簡介

余麗婷為自由插畫家，作品常見於國語日報、聯合報等，自寫自畫《家有怪物》曾獲第四屆國語日報牧笛獎。非常喜歡拍照和旅行。

她用壓克力顏料創作小怪獸系列，認為怪獸世界是充滿無限想像的。最想知道怪獸要怎麼用三隻爪子來蓋房子；最想把怪獸的爪子拿來做成餅乾造型，然後暢銷全世界。

Monster Series 小怪獸系列

學習英文0～2年者（國小1～3年級）適讀

世界上真的有怪獸嗎？
雖然他們有像恐龍一樣突起的背脊
和尖尖的牙齒，
但是他們卻有一顆善良的心 ——
紅鼻子怪獸收留了鄰居的小貓，
紫腳趾怪獸教妹妹寫作業，
電視壞掉了，卻發現更有趣的事……

—— 一起來探索怪獸的世界吧！

—— 小怪獸系列有三本，皆附中英雙語CD ——

1. The TV Is Mine!
   電視是我的！

2. I Hate Homework
   我討厭寫作業

3. A Monster Surprise
   小怪獸的驚喜

文／Jill McDougall
圖／余麗婷

國家圖書館出版品預行編目資料

The TV Is Mine!:電視是我的! / Jill McDougall著;余麗
婷繪.－－初版二刷.－－臺北市：三民，2015
　面；　　公分.－－(Fun心讀雙語叢書.小怪獸系列)
中英對照
ISBN 978－957－14－4680－6　　(精裝)

1. 英國語言－讀本

523.38　　　　　　　　　　　　　　　95025207

© The TV Is Mine!

——電視是我的！

著 作 人	Jill McDougall
繪　　者	余麗婷
發 行 人	劉振強
著作財產權人	三民書局股份有限公司
發 行 所	三民書局股份有限公司
	地址　臺北市復興北路386號
	電話　(02)25006600
	郵撥帳號　0009998-5
門 市 部	(復北店) 臺北市復興北路386號
	(重南店) 臺北市重慶南路一段61號
出版日期	初版一刷　2007年1月
	初版二刷　2015年1月
編　　號	S 806901

行政院新聞局登記證局版臺業字第○二○○號

有著作權·不准侵害

ISBN　978-957-14-4680-6　　(精裝)

http://www.sanmin.com.tw　三民網路書店